DEPRESSION

Cathie Cush

RSVP

RAINTREE
STECK-VAUGHN
PUBLISHERS

The Steck-Vaughn Company

Austin, Texas

Consultants:
Marilyn Devroye, Consultant; Psychiatric Institute of America
Kathy M. Yost, Social Worker; Family Service Association of Bucks County, PA

Developed for Steck-Vaughn Company by Visual Education Corporation, Princeton, New Jersey
Project Director: Jewel Moulthrop
Editors: Dale Anderson, Paula McGuire
Editorial Assistant: Carol Ciaston
Photo Research: Cindy Cappa

Raintree Steck-Vaughn Publishers staff
Editor: Gina Kulch
Project Manager: Joyce Spicer
Electronic Production: Scott Melcer
Photo Editor: Margie Foster

Library of Congress Cataloging-in-Publication Data
Cush, Cathie, 1957-
       Depression / Cathie Cush.
          p. cm—(Teen hot line)
       Includes index.
       Summary: Deals with a variety of issues related to teenage depression, including personal relationships and pressures, substance abuse, suicide, running away, and how to get help and develop coping skills.
       ISBN 0-8114-3529-6
       1. Depression in adolescence—Juvenile literature. (1. Depression, Mental.)
I. Title. II. Series.
       RJ506.D4C9   1994
       616.85′27′00835—dc20   93-14252
                                                                CIP   AC

Photo Credits: Cover: © Brent Peterson/The Stock Market; 18: Steve Takatsuno/ The Picture Cube; 25: Laimute E. Druskis/Photo Researchers, Inc.; 28: Blair Seitz/ Photo Researchers, Inc.; 36: Cleo Freelance Photo/The Picture Cube; 40: Michael Austin/Photo Researchers, Inc.; 49: William Thompson/The Picture Cube; 53: © David Young Wolfe/PhotoEdit.; 58: Dorothy Littell/Stock Boston; 70: Mark Richards/PhotoEdit; 75: Robert Brenner/PhotoEdit

CONTENTS

What Teen Hot Line Is All About 4

Interview 6

Bulletin Board 12

Chapter 1: Communicating 14

Chapter 2: A Time for Changes 22

Chapter 3: Feeling Bad 30

Chapter 4: Reaching Out 38

Chapter 5: Substance Abuse: Not a Solution,
    Just Another Problem 47

Chapter 6: Running Away 55

Interview 62

Chapter 7: The Pain of Suicide 68

Where to Go for Help 76

For More Information 78

Index 79

What the

Teen Hot Line

Is All About

This book is like a telephone hot line. It answers questions about depression that may puzzle you. Answering them requires us to give you the facts. You can use those facts to make your own decisions about what to do if you think that you—or someone you know—may be suffering from depression. Think of us as the voice on the phone, always there to answer your questions, even the ones that are hard to ask.

Just so you know where we stand, here is a list of what we think teens should do when they or someone they know might be depressed. These steps are based on common sense and finding out facts. They assume that you want to make your own decisions and that you want to behave responsibly.

1 Find out everything you can about depression by reading this book and other books.

2 Talk to others to get information you need. These can include friends, brothers and sisters, parents, other adults you can confide in, and people who are trained to help those suffering from depression.

3 Remember that depression is not a permanent problem or a sign of weakness. Someone who is depressed needs help, just like someone who is physically ill. With care, he or she can recover from it.

4 Remember that using drugs or alcohol is not a solution but can become another problem.

5 If a friend tells you that he or she is considering suicide, tell a responsible adult. Your friend needs help.

After you read the book, we hope that you will have some answers to your questions and perhaps to some questions you hadn't even thought of yet. At the back of the book is a list of sources for more information. Thinking about the issues raised in this book is an important step toward taking control of your own life.

Interview

Steve is 18 years old and still under treatment for manic-depressive illness. Although Steve's illness is less common than major depression, many of his experiences—deep depression, suicide attempts, hospitalization—are similar to those of people with other depressive illnesses.

Today, Steve is a college freshman. But when he was in high school, he was so depressed that he had to be hospitalized. In this interview, he described his illness and how he learned to cope with it.

The worst time in my life was my junior year in high school. I had a couple of problems, and I wound up in the hospital for a little while. It happened in early October. I just stopped sleeping.

Part of my problem was biological. I've been diagnosed with *manic-depressive illness*. It's extreme mood swings. When you're manic, you feel like you have more energy than you know what to do with. You feel like you can do absolutely anything, no matter what, no matter how unrealistic. It's being really hyper. You have so many ideas and plans going around in your head, and you just keep getting more. The whole time, you never think anything's wrong with you.

Then you get depressed. It's the total opposite. No energy at all. You think you're at the bottom of the heap and you'll never get up. The world seems like a real bad place, and you feel like you're only making it worse.

When you're manic-depressive, you swing between feeling one way or the other. Some people have in-between periods. There were no in-betweens for me. I would be manic for a few months, then depressed for a few months. Other people's cycles can be much longer or shorter. Some people cycle every few days.

There were some emotional things, too. I was always more interested in books and school than in sports and girls. I didn't really feel like I fit in with the rest of the guys, and you know how mean kids can be when somebody's different. I didn't have a lot of friends.

Anyway, by my junior year I started to take on a lot more activities than I would normally. I was in some advanced placement classes to begin with, and when school began, I started working two jobs. I kept putting extra pressure on myself. I always thought I could do more, that I should do more. I was out of control. Within about a month, I had stopped sleeping. Looking back, I probably behaved strangely in other ways, too, but nobody said anything to me. And I didn't tell anyone that I was having a problem, because I didn't want anyone to see that I could fail.

I lost a lot of weight. Then—literally overnight—I went from being manic to being depressed. I still remember exactly when it happened. We had gone to pick pumpkins. The day before, everything was great. But then I got depressed. At the pumpkin farm, I saw this other family that obviously wasn't as well off as mine. If I had been manic, I probably wouldn't even have noticed them. Instead, I felt so guilty about it. I felt like I was an awful person because they were poor. The feeling didn't go away. A few days later, I stopped getting out of bed.

My mother took me to a therapist. She had taken me to this therapist when I was 13 and having some trouble about my parents' divorce. The approach that the therapist took didn't address my biological problem and didn't really help me deal with my sense of identity. The therapist was working more on how I felt from day to day and telling me things I could do to feel better, but that didn't get to the root of my problems.

I went to the therapist from November until January, but I got worse. I started cutting myself with sharp things and getting into pot and cocaine. I swung between self-loathing and not feeling anything. Then in January, I started going to a psychiatrist who put me on medication to help the biological part of my problem. The medication didn't start to work right away, and in the middle of February, I sliced my wrist. That's when I was first admitted to the hospital. I was there for a few days until the crisis was over. I was hospitalized three times that spring. Twice it was because I had swallowed some pills, and the last time, I was in for cutting my face.

A psychiatric hospital is a hard place to be in, but I needed to be there to let off some steam. You don't know anyone, so you might feel real alone, but it's also a pretty supportive environment. The other patients there are in the same shape you are, so you sort of stick together and try to help each other. In a way, you feel like they understand you better than the kids at school do, because they're going through it, too.

I was in a small, private hospital. It wasn't too structured, and I could go back to my room to read if I wanted to. We had group talks and some individual therapy, and we did things like arts and crafts. You look back at some of the things, and they seem pretty silly. But if you're honest, you realize you're not capable of doing much else then. You're impaired. Arts and crafts are about all you can handle.

We were allowed to do solitary activities, which is valuable. I was kind of surprised, because before, I was always hearing that I spent too much time alone. In the hospital, the situation's different. You're in an environment where all pressures are off you. It's good that you can be left alone to do some reflecting. It was pretty frightening, I mean, the realization that I had come to that point where I couldn't take care of myself.

A couple of times that spring, the doctor switched my medication until we found something that controlled my depression without giving me too many side effects like feeling tired all the time, or thirsty. I was still seeing a therapist, but therapy couldn't do much until I got the biological problem under control with the medication. The therapist would work on helping me modify my thoughts, you know, lighten up on myself. But until the doctor got my brain chemistry under control, I didn't know which thoughts were accurate and which weren't.

Fortunately, through all this I had a real good guidance counselor from my school, who put me on a homebound study program. I was able to keep up as much as I could and graduate on time. I had always been a good student, and everyone at school went out of their way to help me finish and graduate.

One of the things my junior year taught me is that I know nothing is ever going to be so bad for me that I can't deal with it. I've had some problems since then, but I know what to look for. For instance, I know if I start to get extremely organized, it's a sign that I'm getting manic again.

The other thing is that I learned to take care of myself—like taking my medication when I'm supposed to. I guess that's part of growing up. You have to learn to take care of yourself. I had a couple of manic-depressive episodes in college this year. I coped with them better each time, because I was able to deal with the emotions. You learn not to give in to the mood.

When I was in high school, I didn't know anything about manic-depression. So when it hit, it threw me for a loop. My parents had gone to a marriage counselor, so the idea of getting professional help wasn't strange in our family. If I hadn't known that it was OK to go to therapy, I think it would have been much worse for me. I was fortunate. Also, I wasn't afraid of rejection from my parents. I knew I could count on my family, and that's important. And I'm the youngest of four children, so my parents had mellowed out a lot by the time they got to me. I'm sure growing up was much harder for my oldest sister, who's nine years older than me.

Some of the kids at school ignored what was happening with me, and some were mean about it. They'd say,

"Oh, he's crazy." That might have been worse if I were in junior high. Kids can be really mean at that age. It's hard not to judge other people and not to judge yourself. You don't know why a person does X, Y, or Z. You can only see things your own way, through your own filters. That happens whether or not you're aware of it. You judge people so quickly as you're growing up. People are just so severe with other people.

When you're a teen, kids tell you to do your own thing and ignore everyone else. That's not possible. But you do have to start learning what works for you and understand that everyone is different—that you're an individual. Your expectations will be different from what your friends and your parents expect from you.

Kids need to learn to make their own decisions, but they don't always know what their options are. I was lucky. My parents were always telling us to go our own way. But not all teens are ready to accept each other as individuals. I knew a couple of people that I admired who did their own thing, but they were mostly ignored by everyone. It was hard for me to feel good, even with the support network I had. People are hard on themselves.

I've started to mature in a lot of ways. I see a big difference between how I was two years ago and how I am today. I've learned to listen to myself. I've become much more responsible. And I've learned to accept myself for who I am. You have to see what you are—not what your older brother or someone else is.

BULLETIN BOARD

Depression and Mental Disorders

Number of people under 18 admitted to residential treatment programs of mental health organizations in the U.S. in 1990: 29,595

Percent of patients who are under 18 admitted to private psychiatric hospitals: 12

Number of people under 18 in the U.S. estimated to have some mental disorder: 7.5-14 million (12-22 percent)

Number of children and adolescents who receive treatment for mental disorders: 2 million

Amount spent annually on treatment for child and adolescent mental disorders in the U.S.: $1.5 billion

Percent of depressive disorders that can be managed successfully: 80-90

	Number of Suicides for Year	Number of Suicides Each Day
1986	5,120	14.0
1987	4,924	13.5
1988	4,929	13.5
1989	4,870	13.3
1990	4,869	13.3

Source: U.S. National Center for Health Statistics.

Suicides are not always reported as such. Many deaths due to accidents, drug overdoses, and similar causes may actually be suicides. Most experts believe that statistics based on reported suicides may be low and do not reflect the scope of the problem.

Suicide

Number of suicides in the U.S. in 1990: 30,906

Rank of suicide as cause of death for teenagers and young adults: 3

Number of suicides completed by people ages 15-24 in the U.S. in 1990: 4,869

Number of deaths by suicide per 100,000 for young people ages 15-24 in 1950: 4.5

Number of deaths by suicide per 100,000 for young people ages 15-24 in 1989: 13.3

Highest suicide risk group: white males ages 15-19

Percent of people with no history of mental disorders who attempt suicide: 1

Percent of those with major depression who attempt suicide: 18

Estimated number of adolescents who attempt suicide each year: 500,000

Percent of actual suicides by teens who have made previous attempts: 80

Percent of teens who attempt suicide who lost a parent before age 14: 80

Percent of teens who attempt suicide who come from broken homes: 44-66

Sources: *Einstein Health Update.* Albert Einstein Healthcare Foundation, 1993.

Monthly Vital Statistics Report. Centers for Disease Control and Prevention/National Center for Health Statistics, Vol. 40, No. 7S, January, 1993.

National Plan for Research on Child and Adolescent Mental Disorders. U.S. Department of Health and Human Services, National Institute of Health, 1990.

National Runaway Switchboard. Brochure and Fact Sheet, 1992.

Statistical Abstract of the United States, 1992. U.S. Department of Commerce.

10 Myths About Mental Health. Friends Hospital. June, 1992.

CHAPTER 1

Communicating

Q Sometimes I feel real messed up inside. I don't know why; I just do. Like I'm a big nothing, and nothing I do ever goes right. I can't talk to anybody about it, because no one can understand how I feel. What should I do?

A Believe it or not, talking is the best thing you *can* do. Talking about your feelings is one of the best ways to understand them and to keep them from overwhelming you. Sometimes you may not be sure exactly how you feel. By trying to put your feelings into words, you can better understand your emotions. And by learning to express your feelings instead of holding them inside, you can prevent them from causing you serious problems.

• • • • • • • • • • • •

Q But isn't it better not to think about your problems? Doesn't feeling sorry for yourself just make it worse?

A There's a big difference between feeling sorry for yourself and trying to understand your feelings. "Keeping a stiff upper lip" and hiding your feelings aren't helpful. Let's say one of your teachers makes a joke at your expense, and you think that what he or she said was cruel. You'd probably be very angry. If you ignore your anger, you might end up taking it out on someone else. Or, even worse, you might blame yourself and become depressed.

Q Are you saying it's OK to be angry with my teachers?

A I'm saying that there are no right or wrong feelings. Anger is a natural feeling—one of a wide range of emotions that we all experience. But there are right and wrong ways of expressing those feelings. Talking back to your teacher when you are upset is wrong. Explaining your feelings to your teacher is OK. Part of growing up is learning how to express your feelings in an acceptable manner.

Q But sometimes I'm not sure what I feel. What do I do then?

A Talking helps then, too. Talking can help you pinpoint your real feelings—to get a handle on them so you can understand them. But it's not always easy to know who to talk to or where to begin. A hot line like this one is a good start if you don't know where else to turn.

When you were an infant, you were very good at letting those around you know when you were hungry or happy or tired. Now that you're a teenager, your needs are more complex. They are tied to your emotions—and expressing them is not so simple. Learning to identify and understand your emotions and to communicate them effectively and appropriately to others are important skills. They are skills that you'll use for the rest of your life.

Learning to handle your emotions is important for several reasons:

■ Handling your emotions can help you interact more effectively with others—friends, teammates, teachers, parents, or employers.

■ Handling your emotions can help identify you as a mature teen who is moving toward adulthood.

■ Recognizing and talking about anger, sadness, frustration, and other negative feelings can help to keep them from getting the better of you and leading to bigger problems. One of those problems is depression.

For many teens—and even adults—learning to recognize and talk about feelings is difficult. It is a skill that needs to be learned and practiced. Let's look at some ways that might help make it easier.

Sorting Out Your Feelings

Teens experience a wide range of complicated emotions that can change very quickly. Some feelings will be familiar, and others will be brand new. You might feel excited, sad, angry, happy, guilty, loving, nervous, confident, insecure, affectionate, disappointed, proud, annoyed, insulted, hateful, playful, or confused.

The list could go on and on, but it gives you an idea of how many different emotions you can feel. As you work on identifying your feelings, try to be specific. If you feel bad, ask yourself questions. Are you disappointed that you didn't make the team? Are you resentful because you think you got cut unfairly? Are you angry with yourself because you made a bad play during the tryouts? You can feel more than one emotion at a time. Figuring out how you feel is the first step toward being able to talk about your emotions.

Some teens don't stop to think about their own emotions. Instead, they focus on how people around them feel. This is especially true if a teen has a parent with a serious problem. These teens may spend more time worrying about the parent than they spend caring for their own emotional needs. But neglecting those needs can have serious results.

Stephanie was a good student until her junior year. Then her grades dropped suddenly. "My grades were always good because I never went out," Stephanie said sadly. "I stayed home to be company for my mom, who was always sick. My dad left us a long time ago."

A concerned teacher suggested that Stephanie visit the school psychologist to sort out her feelings. Stephanie insisted that nothing was wrong, but her teacher persisted, and she finally agreed to go. The more she talked to the psychologist, the clearer it became that she was angry with her mother. Doing poorly in school was a way of punishing her mother, who valued good grades.

"If I hadn't talked to Dr. MacAfee, I never would have seen how angry I was or what I was doing," Stephanie said. "Being able to understand what I was feeling and admit to someone that I was angry with my mother helped me deal with it."

With this new understanding, Stephanie was able to work on her real problem. She convinced her mother to let her date. She found that with her new social life, her whole attitude improved. And her grades improved as well. Stephanie learned that it's not selfish to take time to focus on her own feelings.

Like Stephanie, you might not be clear about your feelings right away, either. If not, try writing them down on paper. If something happened to make you feel a certain way, write a story about it. Make yourself the main character. Or write a poem—paint a picture with words. How do you feel? How long have you felt this way? What does it remind you of?

Doing poorly in school may be a sign of a deeper problem. A trusted teacher or guidance counselor may be able to help you find a solution or refer you to another professional who can.

You could also write a letter. You could address it to the person who made you feel this way or to a friend. You don't have to send the letter, unless you decide to. Another option is to keep a diary. Anne Frank, a young Jewish girl, became famous for the diary she kept while her family hid from the Nazis during World War II. Writing in her diary gave her a way to express her feelings of sadness, loneliness, and fear during this terrible time.

No matter what approach you take, the important thing is that you learn to recognize and understand your feelings. No one else needs to see the things you write. But you can use the writing to explore your feelings and get a better understanding of yourself. Sometimes simply expressing the angry thoughts improves your mood.

T.J., 16, was shattered when he heard that his girlfriend,

Kendra, liked somebody else. He wanted to call her but didn't know what to say. He wrote her a letter instead. "I said everything I was feeling right then, and some of it was pretty nasty," T.J. recalled. "I read it over a couple of times, then stuck it in a drawer. I left it there for a couple of days and then read it again before I talked to Kendra."

T.J. decided to say some of the things he had written in the letter and not others. "I was upset, but I still cared about Kendra and didn't want to hurt her feelings. Besides, I didn't think that being nasty would get her back," he explained. "Writing the letter was a good way to get the anger out and calm down before I called her. When we did talk, we were able to do it without the anger. We ended up going our separate ways, and feeling OK about it."

Word of Mouth

Writing about your emotions is one way to sort them out and express them. Another is talking. Teens talk to many different people. Some talk to their parents. Others talk to a brother or sister or a best friend. Coaches, teachers, guidance counselors, and ministers or rabbis are other good people to talk to.

The important thing is to find someone you trust and whose judgment you respect. You'll want that person to keep what you reveal confidential. You'll want to know that he or she is really listening and understands what you're saying. You'll want to know that he or she respects your feelings. Someone who makes your feelings seem foolish or unimportant is not going to help you very much.

Talking to someone else does a couple of things for you. It helps you sort your feelings out and lets you express them. What's more, another person can offer you a different way of looking at a situation; or they might suggest a solution that had not occurred to you. And, most important, sharing your troubles makes you feel less alone.

Confronting a Problem

Sometimes talking to another person about how you feel or expressing your feelings on paper is enough. At other times, you need to solve the problem or change the situation that is making you feel bad. In some cases, this requires talking to a person who may also be involved in the situation. There are some steps you can take that will make it easier for both of you:

■ Let the other person know that you have something to discuss, and arrange a time for both of you to talk about it. It's not fair to the other person to insist on settling things right then and there. It will only catch him or her off guard—making that person unnecessarily defensive. You'll accomplish a lot more if you wait until you're both ready to communicate.

Choose a time and place that's appropriate for serious talking. Make sure that you and the other person have plenty of time and won't be interrupted.

■ When the time comes to talk, stay as calm as possible. Use words to convey how you feel rather than gestures or tone of voice. Then the other person will be more receptive to what you have to say. If you are yelling or crying or being abusive, most people will shut you out without listening to you.

■ Use "I" sentences to make your point without attacking the other person. For example, say, "I'm really disappointed about not making the team; I thought I had a pretty good chance," instead of "You were unfair when you selected the team." Or "I miss the time we used to spend together after school," instead of "You don't want to be friends anymore!" This way, you are simply stating a fact—how you feel—without accusing the other person of doing something bad. And the other person can talk about the issue without feeling that it's necessary to defend him- or herself first.

■ When it's the other person's turn to talk, *listen* carefully. Whether it's your dad, who thinks you should do more chores before you borrow the family car, or a friend who cancelled plans with you at the last minute, the other person has reasons and feelings, too. Listen and try putting what they say in your own words to make sure you understand.

When two people are really listening to each other, it's easier to resolve the problem between them. In order for this to happen, they must learn to recognize their feelings and be able to communicate them clearly and maturely. This process takes practice and experience—for both teens and adults.

Growing up is often a confusing and painful experience. It can be even more confusing if you let your emotions whirl around you without trying to understand them. And it can be even more painful if you keep those confusing thoughts and emotions to yourself. Remember, there are many people who care about you and who can help you. Talking to yourself (on paper) or to others (aloud) can help you sort out the confusion and ease the pain.

CHAPTER 2

A Time for Changes

Q I'm 16, and my mother is driving me crazy. One minute she's yelling at me about being responsible, and the next she's telling me what to wear to school. She expects me to act like I'm 40, but she treats me like I'm 4. How can I make her see me like the 16-year-old I am?

A It can be frustrating to feel that you're being treated as a child though you're expected to act as an adult. It doesn't seem fair. You probably feel pretty mature now, and in many ways you are. You're exploring new relationships and making choices that will affect your future. You may even be working and earning your own money. At the same time, you are still your parents' child. If you're like most teens, you still rely on them to pay most of the bills and to keep a roof over your head. It sounds as though your mom is frustrated, too. She may not fully understand your need to make your own decisions. Probably she wants to see more "adult behavior" before she treats you as you think she should. Instead of getting angry at each other, try talking about what each of you expects or wants from the other.

• • • • • • • • • • •

Adolescence is possibly the most confusing time in anyone's life. In a few short years, teenagers experience tremendous physical, social, and emotional changes. Your relationships with friends, family, and members of the opposite sex evolve as you develop a sense of who you are. Your interests and goals may change. Hormones, chemicals produced in the body that affect how it functions, cause changes like beard growth and breast development, which mark the onset of adulthood. They can also cause strong shifts in mood that sometimes make you feel out of control. All of these changes are a normal part of growing up.

You and Your Friends

Most young children don't spend time worrying about who they are. Teenagers are usually more introspective—they look inside themselves at what they think and how they feel. They begin to examine their values—what is right and wrong—and decide what is most important to them. They are exposed to more people and more information, and they form opinions about people around them and events in the world. All of these thoughts and feelings shape their identity, their sense of who they are. As teens develop a sense of identity, their relationships with other people change.

"Heidi and I were best friends for as long as I can remember, until this year," said Heather, 15. "Then in September I made the hockey team, so I have practice every day after school. Heidi started hanging around with this group of kids that goes to the mall all the time. I don't have time to do that, and I think it's boring, just walking around the mall. The last couple of times she came over to my house, we didn't have that much to talk about."

At first Heather felt awkward and a little sad at the thought of losing her friend. "Then I realized that it was OK," she explained. "We both have new friends, and we're happy with them. And it's not like Heidi and I are enemies or anything. It's just that we don't have that much in common anymore."

It's not unusual for childhood best friends to grow apart when they reach adolescence and their interests take different directions. It's also common for teen friendships to change rapidly as teens "try on" different types of people to see where they fit in. But some friendships formed in high school last for a very long time.

Same-sex friendships aren't the only ones that change during adolescence. At the same time, relationships with members of the opposite sex become increasingly important to most teens. Young men and women start to look at one another in a new light—as potential romantic partners. For some teens, this change will happen when they are quite young. Others may not feel ready for these kinds of relationships until they are in their late teens or early 20s. Whichever group you fall into, there's no reason to feel weird or abnormal or even immature. It's different for everyone. Generally, girls develop an interest in the opposite sex before boys do, but it really depends on the person. Some teens will date many people and get to know different personality types. Others will settle down early and go steady with someone for a long time.

Because teens change so much during these years, the majority of these relationships don't turn into lifetime partnerships. Sometimes boyfriends and girlfriends just drift apart, like many same-sex friends do. But more often, one member of the couple is ready to end the relationship before the other one. This can really hurt the person who wants to continue the relationship. It may hurt less if the person leaving the relationship explains that his or her needs have changed. That way, the other person doesn't feel as if he or she did something wrong. It also helps for the person "left behind" to remember that no matter how intense the pain, it goes away over time. As a teen, you can look forward to many relationships in your life.

Teens Face Conflicts

Other relationships change for teenagers, too. Many teens, like the hot-line caller at the beginning of this chapter, experience

Parents and their teenage children come into conflict about a variety of issues, such as the teen's growing independence. Both sides need to adjust to their changing relationship.

conflicts with their parents as they start to feel more independent. Parents and teens may disagree about issues such as dress, curfew, music, use of the family car, and dating. Parents may also disapprove of a teenager's new friends, and they will usually take a stand against drinking, drugs, or dropping out of school.

It has been said countless times, but it's worth saying again: Parents make the rules they do because they care about their children. It's hard for teens to see very far into the future, so they don't always understand the consequences of their actions.

Tom, 19, dropped out of school three years ago, against his parents' wishes. Now he is studying for the General Educational Development test (also known as the high school equivalency diploma, or GED) and hoping to get into a junior college.

"I thought I knew better than my parents. After all, they hadn't been in school in 25 years," he said. "I was bored. I wanted to get out and start making money. Hah! That was a joke. I got a factory job, but I worked nights, so I never saw my friends. Then the place laid a bunch of us off," he continues. "I've been floating around at minimum-wage jobs ever since. It stinks. If I had listened to my dad, I would have gone to voc-tech school. I could be doing electronics repair now, and making decent money."

Sometimes parents get very angry. That doesn't mean they don't care. In some cases, the anger comes from their having a hard time with the changing relationship, too. They are not used to their children questioning or disobeying their rules. It may be hard for them to get used to thinking of you as a young adult with a mind of your own. They may be very concerned about something you are doing, or they could be frightened for your well-being.

Your adolescence can be an emotional time for them, too. You may feel responsible for yourself, but they still feel responsible for you. That's not likely to change, no matter what you say to them. When you're feeling frustrated and angry with your parents, it helps to talk to them so that you can each try to understand the other's perspective.

Much the same can be said for teachers and other authority figures. You're at or near a point in your life where you feel that you can talk to them on an equal level. You may start to question them, which you probably never did as a child. The more mature you are in your dealings with adults, the sooner they are likely to recognize you as someone who can think for him- or herself.

Other Pressures

Trying to make sense of all your changing relationships can be difficult. It's even harder because teens have to deal with other pressures at the same time. In elementary school, grades aren't a big issue, but it's different with teens. The majority say that grades are their main concern. In high school, good grades make a big difference when it comes to getting into college or earning a scholarship. Teachers and guidance counselors are glad to help if you feel that your grades aren't what they should be. They can arrange for tutoring or develop a study plan for you.

If you feel that you didn't receive a grade you deserved, talk to your teacher about it. Bring copies of tests, papers, or projects that you think should have earned you a higher grade. The teacher can explain why you received the grade you did and how your work needs to improve. Sometimes your teacher will change his or her mind or recommend extra work that you can do to raise your grade. Sometimes you'll have to accept the original grade. If so, listen to what the teacher says you need to do better—and work on it.

Unfortunately, teenagers occasionally run into unfair situations at school, on teams, or at work. Sometimes you can help the other person see your point of view by talking it over, and sometimes you can't. Feeling powerless is a big reason why many teens are angry and frustrated.

In that situation, the best step is to talk the problem out with someone else—someone you like and someone who will listen to you sympathetically. Sometimes just talking about anger, frustration, sadness, loneliness, pressure, and other feelings helps you feel better. It is easier to handle these emotions if you have a strong sense of self-esteem—a good feeling about who you are. It also helps not to spend too much time focusing on feeling bad. Often, feeling sorry for yourself can make you feel worse. Learning to handle your emotions is an important aspect of taking charge of your life.

It helps teens to have a support network—people they can talk to if they have a problem or just feel down. It could be anybody—an older brother or sister; a parent or other relative; a good friend, a coach, or a favorite teacher—anyone who cares enough to listen. A lot of people want to help, because they know what it's like to be a teenager. Just ask.

Taking Care of Yourself

When you were a child, your parents and teachers took care of you. As a teenager, you are beginning to be responsible for yourself. Taking good care of yourself physically and emotionally puts you in a better position to deal with the changes of adolescence. Your health can affect your outlook, and your emotions can influence how you feel physically. As a teen, you have more control over your schedule and your diet than you did as a child. These are some ways to help maintain your health:

■ Make sure to get enough sleep (eight hours) and eat right (a balanced diet).

■ When you're tempted to snack, make it a healthful one—such as fruit or carrot sticks.

■ Exercise is important, too. Research indicates that regular exercise stimulates endorphins, chemicals in the blood that help you feel good. Joining an athletic team is one way to get exercise. It's also a good way to get to know new people and to feel a part of something. If you don't care for team sports like football, softball, or field hockey, you might prefer to get involved in tennis, track, swimming,

It's important to take good care of your physical and emotional health. Exercise stimulates chemicals in the blood that help people feel good.

bicycling, or karate. These sports can be good exercise and lots of fun, and they don't have to be competitive.

■ If you're not athletic, you can find other ways to get involved. You might try out for the school play or volunteer to paint scenery. You could help tutor younger students, or become involved in community service—working at a local animal shelter or volunteer fire company.

Whatever you choose, the payoff can be great. That's what Josh found out. "Nothing was going right my sophomore year," he recalled. "My best friend moved away, and I didn't make the wrestling team. I really liked this one girl, but she didn't like me. I really felt like a loser. I started just coming home and sitting in my room after school. It was pretty lousy."

Josh's older brother, Mark, knew something wasn't right, and he got Josh to talk about it. He suggested that Josh volunteer at the local hospital, where Mark was learning to be a physical therapist. Josh agreed to give it a try. Now, two afternoons a week, he brings mail to patients' rooms and runs errands for the nurses.

"At first I thought it was going to be bogus, but it's pretty cool. The nurses are super nice to you, 'cause you really help them," Josh said. "And when you see all those sick people, you realize you don't have it so bad. But the best part was meeting Janine. She goes to a different school, but volunteers the same days I do. We're dating now."

Josh learned that he wasn't going to feel any better brooding by himself. Simply by taking action and feeling useful, he began to feel better about himself and his life.

The most important thing for teens to remember is that strong emotions are normal anytime there is so much change. Taking care of yourself, getting involved with others, and communicating your feelings can make your emotions seem less overwhelming.

CHAPTER 3

Feeling Bad

Q My name's Seth. I'm 15. I used to do pretty well in school, but lately it doesn't seem worth trying. What's the point? Sometimes I can't even make myself go to class. I'll just sit in the library and flip through dumb magazines. What's wrong with me?

A From what you're saying, it sounds as though you've felt "down" for some time. Everybody gets the blues once in a while, and sometimes those feelings can last for a few days. But when feelings of sadness, emptiness, or hopelessness last a week or more, it may be a sign of a serious depression. Calling and asking for help was the right thing to do. With guidance from a professional, most cases of depression can be resolved. Too many depressed teens suffer needlessly, because they don't realize that help is available, or they're afraid people may think less of them, or they feel too bad to do anything for themselves. The important thing is not to give up. With the help of someone else, you can make your life better.

• • • • • • • • • • • •

Depression is a very common mood disturbance that affects different people in different ways at different times. It is a serious health problem, not a sign of weakness or immaturity. Anyone can be depressed. Teens are prone to wide mood swings as they undergo rapid physical changes and face new social stresses. Coping with the pressures of school, part-time jobs, and new responsibilities may lead to depression. It's important to learn to recognize the symptoms of depression in yourself and others, so that you can get help early. With treatment, most depressed people start feeling well again in a few weeks. But if depression isn't treated, it can get much worse. It could lead to drug or alcohol abuse, running away, or possibly even suicide.

"It's hard to explain how bad it feels," said Thomas, 17. "My friends all seem like jerks. I'd be at a party, and all of a sudden I'd just start thinking about how I didn't belong there, not with all those people having a good time. My dad kept telling me to grow up and stop feeling sorry for myself, but I couldn't help it. It wasn't like just being in a bad mood."

Thomas eventually talked to a guidance counselor, who recognized the signs of depression. Thomas now sees a psychologist once a week to help him sort out his feelings. "I wouldn't say that everything is great yet. I've still got a lot of anger and frustration. But I feel a whole lot better than before. I can even laugh again."

Signs of Depression

Everybody gets "the blues" once in a while. You may be feeling lonely or worried about your friends rejecting you or about problems in your family. You may feel irritable and impatient with yourself and people around you. You may not be able to sleep. When this happens from time to time, it's normal. And the feelings usually go away in a few days. A change of pace or a special activity—like a weekend trip or a new exercise program—can often help to chase the blues away.

Serious depression lasts weeks, months, or longer. The pain and feeling of hopelessness are more intense. A depressed teen may lose interest in friends and activities that he or she used to enjoy. He or she may act differently in other ways, too. In very

Types of Depression

Minor Depression

Causes: breakup of a relationship, loss of job, failure in school

Symptoms: sadness, anxiety, crying, pessimism

Major Depression

Causes: trauma such as death in the family, parental divorce, drug or alcohol abuse, hormonal imbalance, heredity

Symptoms: intense feelings of sadness, helplessness, insomnia, loss of self-esteem, guilt, headaches, lethargy, loss of appetite

Manic-Depressive Illness

Causes: unclear, may be due to heredity

Symptoms: extreme euphoria, hyperactivity (manic stage); deep sadness, loss of interest in life (depressive stage)

Source: *Macmillan Health Encyclopedia, Vol. 5: Emotional and Mental Health.* Macmillan, 1992.

Everyone goes through "blue" periods occasionally. When that feeling lasts a long time, it's important to recognize the symptoms and seek help as soon as possible.

severe cases, the depressed person may lose touch with reality.

Someone who starts acting the following ways may be showing signs of depression:

■ Talking about feeling sad, empty, hopeless, helpless, guilty, or worthless.

■ Looking at the negative side of things.

Having a hard time concentrating, remembering things, or making decisions.

Having problems that didn't exist before with school, family, or relationships.

Having trouble falling asleep, staying asleep, or getting up in the morning.

Sleeping or eating much more than usual.

Lacking energy or interest in doing things that one previously enjoyed.

Gaining or losing weight without trying.

Being careless about one's appearance.

Complaining of headaches, stomachaches, backaches, or other pains.

Acting restless and grouchy and wanting to be alone most of the time.

Cutting classes.

Drinking alcohol excessively or taking drugs.

Talking about death or suicide.

We all know someone who likes to sleep late in the mornings or who doesn't really care how he or she is dressed. These actions aren't necessarily a sign of depression. But when someone shows one of these signs—and that behavior is unusual for that person—it could be a sign of something serious.

If you notice that a friend has started acting differently and it continues for more than a few days, be alert to a possible problem. Get your friend to talk about it. Suggest that he or she get help. Follow up. If your friend doesn't go for help, you should alert an adult whom you trust. This is especially important if your friend talks about death or suicide. Such talk is a potential sign of a serious problem that should not be ignored.

Many teens worry about betraying the confidence of a friend if they tell an adult when they've heard these kinds of expressions from a friend. Any time a teen talks about suicide, it is crucial to tell someone else. That person needs help. This isn't betraying a friend's trust; it can save the friend's life.

"Maureen told me that the reason she dropped out of the play was because Jerry broke up with her," confided Karyn. "I knew she was taking it hard. She said she couldn't bear to live without Jeremy, but she made me promise not to tell anyone because she'd be embarrassed. Her folks didn't like Jerry anyway, so they wouldn't understand. About a week later, I heard that she was in the hospital. She had swallowed a whole bottle of aspirin. I felt awful that I hadn't told anybody. What if she'd died? I'll never do that again."

Causes of Depression

Researchers still don't know all the causes of depression, but they are learning more all the time. Certain factors do seem to increase the likelihood that a person will become depressed, and many depressions may be the result of a combination of these things. As researchers study these factors and how they relate to depression, they are able to offer new and better treatments for the depressed.

Biochemistry
One of the most exciting breakthroughs in the study of depression is a new understanding of the role of biochemistry. Researchers now believe that some forms of depression are the result of shortages or imbalances of certain mood-influencing chemicals in the brain. These imbalances may occur naturally, and researchers believe that some are probably hereditary. Depression does seem to run in families. These chemical imbalances may also be caused by certain medications or illnesses.

Fortunately, a number of medications have been developed that seem to restore the brain's natural chemical balance.

Environment

A person's surroundings or certain events can trigger depression. Problems at home might include an alcoholic parent or parents getting divorced. It's common for teens and parents to have problems communicating, and conflicts between parents and teens are another possible cause for depression. In such situations, a teen may feel isolated, with no one to turn to.

The school environment is especially important for teens. Getting accepted into college or finding a good job almost always depends on how well the teen does in school. Most teens feel under pressure to perform in school to different degrees. The pressure may come from family, or the teen may put pressure on him- or herself to do well. That pressure overwhelms some teens. They feel unable to live up to these high expectations. If the expectations are unrealistic, the teen's failure to meet them will only make the teen more depressed.

Specific events, particularly losses, can cause depression. It's normal to be sad when a friend or family member dies or when a relationship ends. Doing poorly on a test and not getting a part in a play or a place on the team can be very disappointing, too. It's natural to feel sad afterward. For a person who is suffering from depression, the hurt feelings grow stronger instead of going away over time. It may seem like the end of the world.

Personality Types

Teens with certain personality traits are more likely to become depressed than others. Teens who are very self-critical or who set excessively high goals for themselves often become depressed. They may expect perfection—from themselves and those around them. The world and the people in it are less than perfect, so these teens are continually disappointed in themselves and others.

Teens, like adults, have a need to feel accepted. School teams, clubs, and other extracurricular activities provide opportunities to join a group that is involved in healthful and enjoyable activities.

Passive, dependent people tend to become depressed more often than active, assertive people do. They feel that they don't have control over their environment or what happens to them. If they're struggling at school, they may blame their problems on teachers who expect too much. If they're unhappy at home, they may think their parents aren't trying hard enough to understand them. They count on others to make them happy.

Getting Help

Whatever the cause, teens who are suffering from depression need help. A depressed person often feels so lost, alone, and overwhelmed that he or she cannot understand the problem well enough to solve it alone. Asking for help is not a sign of weakness; it's a smart choice.

The Role of Self-Esteem

Teens who set realistic goals, who talk openly about their needs and take steps to fulfill them, usually feel good. They value life and themselves. They have high self-esteem. A sense of self-worth makes it easier to handle the pressures of adolescence—or adult life, for that matter. Teens with low self-esteem are more likely to get depressed—and feeling depressed can lower their sense of self-worth even more.

Having high self-esteem isn't being conceited. It's just being realistic about yourself and comfortable with who you are. Teens with high self-esteem have a firm sense of their identity and confidence in their abilities.

Teens who don't feel good about themselves—no matter what the reasons are—can learn to improve their feelings of self-worth. This improvement usually requires some help, whether it's from a book or a trained counselor. With support, it is possible to break the negative thought patterns that lead to low self-esteem and depression.

When Sherri was 16, she contracted a sexually transmitted disease. She went to a local clinic for treatment, and a nurse asked her about her sexual activity. "I had been with a different guy every weekend," Sherri said. "I was so ashamed to admit it. When I told the nurse, I broke down and cried."

The nurse arranged for Sherri to visit a counselor every other week. "We talked about a lot of stuff in counseling," said Sherri. "Like how nothing I ever did was good enough for my mother, so I started believing I was no good. The counselor helped me see I have a lot to offer. Everybody does, really. And the way my mom was treating me was because she didn't feel good about her own self, so she was taking it out on me. It wasn't really my fault. I'm OK." A year later, Sherri was feeling good about herself and had a steady boyfriend.

Maybe the greatest thing about self-esteem is that it seems to have a snowball effect. The better you feel about yourself, the better other people will feel about you. And as they respond to you more positively, you'll feel even better about yourself.

It's not unusual for teens to feel bad, whether it's due to low self-esteem, pressure, or something else. But feeling bad for more than a few days may be a sign of serious depression, and depressed people need help. Learn to recognize signs of depression so you can get help for yourself—or those around you.

CHAPTER 4

Reaching Out

Q Sometimes I feel totally depressed, like my whole life is awful, and I'm not sure why. I read somewhere that a psychiatrist can help with depression, but aren't they only for crazy people? Besides, I'm still in school, so I don't have a lot of money. Do I need help? Where can I get it?

A Yes, you do need help in sorting things out. Psychiatrists are among the many resources available for teens to talk to—and seeing a psychiatrist doesn't mean that you're crazy at all. It means that you're smart enough to ask for help when you need it. If you have a toothache, you see a dentist. If you feel sick, you see a doctor. Why should it be any different when you need help with your feelings?

• • • • • • • • • • • •

It's true that many people don't understand what seeing a mental health professional is all about. A lot of people think that depression is a sign of weakness, but it's not. It's an illness that can be treated like any other. Just like any other illness, depression needs to be treated by a professional. Depressed people cannot cure themselves. Treatment doesn't have to cost a lot of money, either. All over the country there are clinics that can treat people at very low cost. Find out—don't give up just because you're worried about the money.

Everyone goes through some periods when they feel emotionally down. When that feeling goes on for a long time and seems to be affecting the way you behave, you may be depressed. Fortunately, depression can be treated. No one has to suffer without help.

There are many ways to get that needed help. Caring friends and family can help a depressed person somewhat. So can people at school. But what a depressed person really needs is professional care. Only a fully trained and experienced professional can help such a person understand the cause of the depression and help find a solution to the underlying problem. The amount and kind of help a teen needs depend on the severity of the depression.

Friends and Family

Friends and family are an important support network, even when you're not depressed. These are the people you spend the most time with and who know you best. They're likely to notice if something seems wrong with you. Most important, friends and family members care about you. Feeling loved builds self-esteem, and that helps to prevent depression.

Friends and family can help just by being around to listen. If you're down in the dumps, just knowing that someone cares will often lift you up. Friends and family also can offer a different perspective, one that puts things in a different or more positive light.

Keeping active and being with other people can help you get through a down period. Become involved with activities that you used to enjoy, even if you don't feel like it at first. Simply getting back into action can help you feel better.

On the other hand, don't expect too much of yourself, or you may feel overwhelmed. A trip to the mall or the movies with one or two friends would probably be easier to handle than a big party. If many people are having a great time and you aren't, you could wind up feeling even worse.

Friends and family make up a valuable support network. They can often help just by being there to listen, and sometimes to offer a different point of view.

Friends and family members can help each other a lot, but they can't do everything. They're not trained to deal with serious depression the way professionals are. Sometimes they are too close to the problem to see it clearly. And sometimes they are part of the problem—when a teen is depressed because a parent is alcoholic, for instance. When that's the case, a professional can help both people talk to each other more easily.

Resources at School

Not everybody feels comfortable talking to a family member about his or her deepest emotions. In that case, it might be easier to turn to a favorite teacher or coach. Unlike teen friends, teachers have been through adolescence already and know what it's all about. They also work with dozens of young people every day. They may be able to suggest solutions based on what they know other teens have done in similar situations.

"I was ready to drop out of school a year ago," said Franklin, a senior. "Mom and Dad were fighting all the time about my father's drinking, and I just wanted to get out of the house."

One day he said something to his basketball coach. "Mr. Snipes said he felt the same way when he was my age. His dad had a drinking problem, too. He told me about a group called Alateen, for kids whose parents drink too much, and he found out where a local chapter met near our school. Even when I can't get to a meeting, I can still talk to Mr. Snipes. It makes it easier to know that I have someone to talk to who knows what I'm going through."

Guidance counselors are another resource at school. They're specially trained to help teens with all sorts of issues. Teens can talk to guidance counselors about:

Problems in classes

Education and career goals

Balancing school and a part-time job

Problems with relationships and in the family

Frequent bad moods

Depression or suicide

Running away

Sexual identity

Pregnancy

Drug or alcohol use

Legal troubles

In other words, teens can usually talk to a guidance counselor about anything at all. Sometimes it's easier to be honest with someone like a guidance counselor, who will keep the conversation confidential, than it is with a nonprofessional who may not. Counselors will not call your parents or teachers unless that's what you want. Knowing that helps many teens become more open about their worries and fears.

Guidance counselors are willing to listen if you just want to talk. They also know what resources are available to help solve your problems.

Professional Resources

There are many people in the community who are trained to help teens handle their emotions. These professionals include psychiatrists, psychologists, and social workers. They use a variety of methods, including talking one-on-one and holding group sessions. Sometimes medication is needed to treat a person with depression. The length of treatment depends on the person and the severity of the problem, but most depressed teens start to feel better after a few weeks of treatment.

The cost of treatment varies, too, but money shouldn't stand in the way of obtaining help. Many state- or county-sponsored programs base their fees on what the patient can afford to pay. Teens and others who don't have much money can usually obtain counseling inexpensively. Ask about payment policies before scheduling a first appointment. Find out if your parents have health insurance that covers treatment. The important thing is not to let a concern about the fee prevent you from asking for help.

Psychiatrists
Psychiatrists are medical doctors who specialize in treating emotional and psychological problems. They treat cases ranging from mild depression to severe mental illnesses such as schizophrenia. Like other medical doctors, psychiatrists can prescribe medication if it is necessary. They are the only mental health professionals who can prescribe medicines.

A psychiatrist will usually start by reviewing the patient's medical history to see if a medical problem might be causing the depression. He or she will also try to determine if depression runs in the family. The doctor will ask how long the teen has been feeling depressed and evaluate how severe the depression is. From this analysis, the psychiatrist will begin to develop a treatment plan.

Treatment may consist of therapy or medication or both. In severe cases, such as attempted suicide, the depressed patient may be admitted to a psychiatric hospital or the psychiatric floor of a general hospital for intensive treatment.

Psychotherapy consists of the depressed teen and the psychiatrist talking about the teen's problems. Sessions are scheduled on a regular basis to maintain progress in the treatment. The meetings could be private—just the doctor and the patient—or the teen could be part of a therapy group. Both approaches are aimed at helping the teen understand his or her feelings and deal with them. Sessions might focus on family relationships or learning specific skills that can be used to overcome the depression.

When the depression is caused by imbalances in brain chemistry, medication is needed. The medicines usually used are antidepressants or mood-stabilizers. They restore the needed balance in brain chemistry, eliminating the depression. These medications can also give the patient more energy to cope with his or her problems.

Like many medications, antidepressants may have side effects. The psychiatrist will advise the patient to watch for such signs as dry mouth or blurred vision. These side effects may indicate a need to change the dosage—or possibly to switch medicines.

People taking antidepressants must also be careful not to drink alcohol or take any other drugs or medications—even over-the-counter medicines. Interactions between these drugs and the antidepressant can have harmful effects. For example, someone who takes both cold remedies and certain antidepressants could develop high blood pressure.

Psychologists

Psychologists are trained to evaluate people for emotional or psychological problems, determine what the problem is, and treat it. They can not prescribe medication, but if they feel that medication may be advisable, they can work with a psychiatrist or other physician. Psychologists use conversation, role playing, and other proven techniques to help their clients identify and understand the causes of their problems. They might focus on the patient's relationships with others as well as on

Stress can be positive (excitement before an important event) or negative (dread before a difficult exam). Many experts believe that the effects of stress have less to do with the type of stress than with how a person reacts to it.

Stress

What is stress?
Stress is the body's response to physical and mental demands made upon it.

Preventing stress
Time management: setting priorities, budgeting time
Regular exercise
Good nutrition

Coping with stress
Positive outlook   Conflict resolution
Relaxation   Support groups
Problem solving   Counseling or therapy

certain behaviors or attitudes that seem to cause problems.

At 17, Geena had never had a boyfriend. The more she thought about it, the more depressed she got, until she stopped going out with her friends at all.

"I guess my mom got pretty worried about me, because she insisted I see this psychologist," Geena said. "At first I was embarrassed to tell her my problems, but she was a really sympathetic lady, and I found it easy to talk to her. She helped me see that whenever I talked to a guy, I'd get really nervous and pull back. That would make him think that I wasn't interested, so he wouldn't ask me out."

The psychologist taught Geena some relaxation techniques that she could use when she was nervous. They role played, or practiced, situations with guys. Geena learned to be more comfortable in these situations. The practice paid off. "I still haven't found anybody special, but I'm dating now," Geena said. "And I don't spend every weekend at home in my room wondering if I'm abnormal."

Some psychologists and psychiatrists may work in private practice. Others work in hospitals, mental health clinics, or community mental health centers.

Social Workers
Family service agencies can help people who have emotional, social, and economic problems. They may have counselors on staff, or they can provide referrals. Social workers provide fast, practical help. They are a good resource in a crisis. For example, after talking with the person, they could find a shelter for an abused teen or help arrange hospitalization for someone who is thinking of suicide. Social workers often work with the entire family to resolve problems. In some cases, once the crisis has passed, a social worker might continue to see the teen, or recommend that the teen see a psychiatrist or psychologist, to treat the underlying problem.

Help Yourself

There are a number of other services that can help teens with emotional problems. They include hot lines and support groups.

Hot Lines

Suicide prevention centers and hot lines are another resource in an emergency. They are staffed by trained volunteers who have a special interest in helping others. Their services are free. When a teen calls, a staff member will listen and try to talk the caller through the crisis. Staffers can also refer callers to outside sources for follow-up.

Support Groups

Support groups provide help for a group of people who suffer from the same problem. Support groups help teens see that they are not alone. In group meetings, teens can share ideas and solutions to problems. Groups meet regularly, and members are sometimes assigned a "buddy" who has already resolved the problem. They can call on this buddy if they need special advice or assistance in a specific situation. Group leaders may be mental health professionals or specially trained volunteers who were once part of the group themselves. These groups are usually free or at a very low cost.

Many types of help for depression and similar problems are readily available. Just look around and ask. Seeking outside help may seem like a difficult step at first, but it's much easier than feeling alone—and it can help to lead you away from your problem.

CHAPTER 5

Substance Abuse: Not a Solution, Just Another Problem

Q Between the pressure at school and my folks fighting at home all the time, I want to scream. I tried talking to my guidance counselor a couple of times, but he's clueless. Getting high makes me feel better, but I don't always have the money. When I can't get high, I feel worse than before. What do I do now?

A You need to get help for your drug problem and your emotional troubles. Many people who abuse alcohol, drugs, or even food do it to ease their emotional pain. They may not even be aware of why they are doing it. It seems to help for a while, but in the long run substance abuse of any kind makes things worse. It leads to problems of its own—physical and emotional problems, money problems, and problems with the law. Each problem makes the others worse.

• • • • • • • • • • •

It doesn't matter whether you started taking drugs because you were depressed or became depressed after you started taking drugs. The treatment is the same. It involves a lot of talking with a counselor to understand why you feel bad and learning how to feel better without relying on taking illegal drugs, drinking alcohol, or eating too much or too little. The key is understanding your feelings.

Often, depressed teens don't recognize their feelings as depression. They may feel unhappy, but are unable to put their feelings into words. They may start acting differently and not be aware of why. They may start having trouble at school or difficulty getting along with people. It might become hard to concentrate in school or at work. In an attempt to make themselves feel better, many teenagers turn to drugs and other substances.

Drugs and Your Body

Many substances change the way you feel physically and/or emotionally. The caffeine in coffee, tea, and cola gives many people a lift. They feel more energetic. Some people say that smoking cigarettes helps them relax. However, when you take coffee away from people who usually drink a lot of it, they feel sluggish and sleepy. Cigarette smokers who try to quit can become very nervous and irritable. Sometimes they replace smoking with eating, and they gain a lot of weight. Caffeine and nicotine are *addictive*—that is, the body gets used to them and craves them. When a person stops using addictive substances, his or her state of mind can be temporarily affected.

The same is true of stronger drugs, although the effects are more extreme. Users can find it difficult, if not impossible, to stop without help of some kind—either counseling or a peer support group such as Alcoholics Anonymous or Narcotics Anonymous. The withdrawal period can be very hard, both physically and emotionally. People who are addicted to certain drugs—heroin, for example—may have to be hospitalized during the withdrawal period.

Although quitting is difficult, it's not impossible. And there's a payoff. Teens—and adults—who stop using addictive drugs feel better. They feel better about themselves and are more in

Many people turn to pills or alcohol to ease their emotional pain. In reality, these substances may add a whole new set of problems to the ones already existing.

control of their lives. The truth is, drugs don't take away the problems a person has. They simply add another problem. To get rid of the original problem, the drug user needs to overcome the drug habit first.

Drugs may take the user's mind off his or her problems for a while. Then again, they might not. It's a myth that drugs and alcohol always make a person feel better. Sometimes they make bad feelings more intense. It's also harder to control feelings of sadness and anger when you're not sober, because many of these substances make you lose your inhibitions. You do things that you would not do otherwise. Many teens who try to take their own lives are drunk or high when they do so.

Risky Business

Even if they don't try to commit suicide, teens who are depressed will often put themselves in some sort of danger, especially when they are intoxicated. Teenagers, just like older people, may occasionally have thoughts of suicide. When they are drunk or high, and their inhibitions are removed, they are at an increased risk of acting impulsively on a suicidal thought—ramming the car into a telephone pole or jumping out the window.

Paul, 21, remembers a close call in his sophomore year. "I was always a daredevil, a real rowdy. I wasn't good in sports like my brother, and I was no honor student like my sister," he recalled. "So I got a reputation for pulling off these outrageous stunts. I guess for me it was a status thing. I was the ringleader. Most of the stuff we did was pretty stupid—dropping eggs on cars from the overpass, spraying graffiti on the water tower, that sort of thing."

One night Paul decided to get more daring:

"A couple of us had polished off a six-pack of beer and wanted more. Some friends of my parents' were out of town, and I knew they usually kept a couple of cases around, so we decided to break in. Well, the neighbors must have seen us trying to find a way in and called the cops. My two friends bolted when they saw the cruiser, but I was already in the garage. I didn't know cops were there until their lights were on me."

The most sobering part, he said, was staring down the barrel of the officer's drawn gun. "I froze, and in that I moment I realized that all the status in the world wasn't worth this."

Because Paul was a first offender, the judge put him on probation and ordered him into a counseling program at a community mental health clinic. "The counselor helped me see that I didn't have a very good image of myself, and that's why I was doing the things I was doing," he said. "If the judge hadn't sent me to counseling, I never would have gone. I thought that was only for psychos, but clinics can help a lot of people."

Another reason that teens like Paul don't go to mental health clinics or take advantage of other community resources is that many don't realize they have a problem. Some have felt bad for so long that they've forgotten there's another way to feel. Others think that they don't have a problem as long as they aren't drunk or high all the time. Depression isn't always that dramatic. Many depressed teens get up and go to classes every day. It often takes a close call—like Paul's arrest—to make them realize that they have a problem.

Food and Mood

Alcohol and drugs are not the only substances that can be abused. Some teenagers abuse food, too, in several different ways. Abusing food may not sound as serious as taking drugs, but some forms of food abuse are just as dangerous.

Overeating
When some teens feel lonely or anxious or empty inside, they turn to food for comfort. This may happen for many reasons.

One reason is that food reminds many people of when they were happy babies and their mothers fed them. Another reason is that the chemicals in food may make people feel certain ways—as drugs do, only much less dramatically. Often, depressed people crave foods that are high in carbohydrates. They want starchy, sugary foods like cakes, cookies, and ice cream. Carbohydrates stimulate certain chemicals in the brain that have a soothing effect.

Overeating causes many problems. It's not healthy, and a teen who becomes overweight puts him- or herself at risk for certain future health problems—diabetes, high blood pressure, or heart attack. And for a teen with low self-esteem, weight gain can make that problem worse. It's hard to feel good about yourself if you don't like the way you look.

If overeating is a problem, a family doctor can prescribe a diet and exercise program to help you lose weight. Weight loss centers can do the same. These programs often include some individual counseling to help you understand why you overeat and how to break the pattern. Check with your doctor before beginning any diet. Even over-the-counter diet pills may cause some unwanted side effects.

Anorexia
Anorexia is a more serious eating disorder. It is much more common among teenage girls than boys, possibly because today's media tell young women they should be thin. Some teenage girls kill themselves trying to live up to the image.

"I was always a straight A student and a cheerleader. But I never thought I had a very good figure," said Aimee. "That's how I wound up with anorexia. In my junior year, I got the female lead in the school play, The Boyfriend. It takes place in the 1920s, and the 'flappers' were all real skinny in those days. I wanted to be perfect in the part, so I went on a diet."

At first Aimee went on a sensible diet, but she didn't lose much weight, because she wasn't heavy to begin with. After a few weeks, she went on a stricter diet, eating only dinner. "And I only forced that down because my parents were around. When rehearsals started running longer, it was a good excuse to skip eating completely. By the time we did the show, I was skinny. But I couldn't stop dieting."

Aimee, who is 5 feet, 6 inches tall, weighed 120 pounds when she started her junior year. By spring break, she weighed only 90 pounds and was still trying to lose weight. "I realize now how sick I was, but at the time I was only worried about looking good for the play. I had a really messed up perception of how I looked. I still thought I looked fat."

A sensible weight loss program should be discussed with a doctor.

Aimee's parents became concerned about their daughter's extreme weight loss and the problems that came with it. She was weak, her hair was dry and brittle, and she stopped menstruating. They took her to a private hospital that had a treatment program for anorexics. By the time she graduated, Aimee was finished with the program and back to a healthy weight for her frame. Most important, she had learned that she didn't have to be incredibly skinny to be attractive.

Bulimia

When people have anorexia, they eventually stop eating. A related problem is bulimia. Bulimic people will eat huge amounts of food (binge), often in secret, then use laxatives or force themselves to throw up (purge). This binge-purge cycle can lead to gum disease, damage to the esophagus, and irregular heartbeat. Sometimes anorexia and bulimia overlap. About 50 percent of all anorexics develop some symptoms of bulimia.

Like other forms of substance abuse, eating disorders require a thorough medical evaluation before treatment can begin. Successful therapy can't begin until the teen's nutritional balance is restored.

Becoming Well

Drinking, drug abuse, and eating disorders have one thing in common: They are a sure sign that a teen is unhappy with his or her life. This unhappiness may result from low self-esteem or a problem at home or at school. Anyone can experiment with drugs, and no one can predict who will become addicted. But, generally, a person who is happy and emotionally secure won't risk the consequences of getting involved in drugs or feel compelled to live up to an unrealistic idea of perfection.

It's hard to get straightened out on your own. It takes hard work and usually the help of a trained professional. These professionals can't do the work for you, but they can give you the tools you need to take control of your life.

Helping teens with drinking, drug abuse, eating disorders, and other problems that may be caused by depression involves a lot of honesty and communication. Teens in treatment programs learn to recognize their feelings, attitudes, and patterns of behavior that may be troublesome. They learn to express their feelings rather than let their emotions build up and overwhelm them. They learn to accept their weaknesses and build on their strengths and to feel good about themselves.

It's not necessary to wait for a crisis in order to learn and practice these skills. In fact, teens who can recognize and express their feelings and who feel comfortable communicating with those around them are less likely to have problems in the first place. It's also important to seek help at the first sign of a problem. That way you could save yourself and others a lot of unnecessary pain.

CHAPTER 6

Running Away

Q My name's Terri. I don't know what to do. I left home last month because I couldn't stand the way they were treating me any more. I ran out of money, and I've been living with some people in an old warehouse. Yesterday somebody OD'd there. I want to go home. I called, but my stepfather hung up on me. Where do I go from here?

A You *can* get off the streets. And the sooner you do it, the safer and better off you will be. Most large urban communities and many smaller ones offer temporary shelters for people who have nowhere else to go. Going to such a facility would get you out of the dangerous environment of the warehouse until you can get back home. It sounds as though many of the problems that made you leave home may have been with your stepfather. It's not unusual for a teen to have problems adjusting to a stepparent—and vice versa. Have you tried to contact your mother since you left home? It's very likely that she is worried about you and wants you to come home. Can you reach her at a work number or sometime when your stepfather is not at home?

• • • • • • • • • • • •

Another option you have is to turn to a third party. A counselor at a runaway hot line could make the call for you. They're trained to deal with situations like yours. They're not as emotionally involved as you are, so it may be easier for them to talk to your parents. Also, they are aware of other resources that are available to runaway teens. For example, some runaway teens can't or won't go back home but still want to get off the street. A hot-line counselor can put them in touch with agencies that can find a foster home.

More than a million teens live on the streets of America. Although each one left home for a different specific reason, almost all have something in common. They were in situations that made them desperately unhappy. They became so depressed that they felt their only option was to escape from it. They thought a different environment would change everything. Unfortunately, runaways usually encounter a whole new set of problems—those of survival. Let's take a closer look at why teens run away, the problems they face, and some possible solutions and alternatives to running away.

Shattered Families

About 50 percent of the teens who run away do so to escape some sort of abuse—physical, emotional, or sexual. Most often, the abuser is someone who lives in the teen's home. It may be a relative, a parent, a stepparent, or a parent's boyfriend or girlfriend. The teen may not feel able to talk to the other adult in the house about what is happening. Maybe he or she has tried to talk, and did not succeed.

"I tried to tell my mom what her boyfriend was doing to me when she went to work at night, but she didn't believe me. She called me a liar and a whore," said Jill, 17. "She was really crazy about him and didn't believe he could do any wrong. So two years ago, I split."

Jill was on the street for only a week or two when she realized that she couldn't make it on her own. She called her mom to ask if she could come home. "She still didn't really believe what I was saying about her boyfriend, but I guess my leaving made her see that something was really wrong. She worked it out so I could live with my aunt. About six months ago she talked to her boyfriend's ex-wife and found out that he had molested her daughter, and that's why they split up."

Jill's mother broke up with the boyfriend, and now Jill is back at home. "It was kind of awkward at first, but we went to family counseling and got a lot of things out in the open. I see now that she's not perfect and all-knowing. But she's not bad, either. We can support each other now in ways we couldn't before."

In this book, we put strong emphasis on the importance of communication. It's only natural for teens and parents to disagree about many things. But if communication breaks down or stops completely, a teen will feel isolated with nowhere to turn. Some teens run away because they are faced with problems they don't know how to deal with, such as pregnancy, divorce, a move, or the breakup of a friendship or a serious relationship. A teen who feels comfortable turning to his or her parents or other family members is less likely to run away from such a problem.

Another choice Jill might have made was to turn to a third party for help instead of running away. Women's centers, community mental health centers, rape hot lines, and youth shelters can help remove teens from abusive situations. Teens can also report a physically or sexually abusive parent to the police. Ironically, many teens are reluctant to involve the authorities for fear of breaking up the family. Instead, they suffer in silence or run away.

Out of the Frying Pan, into the Fire

Running away from problems doesn't solve them. It doesn't mend a broken relationship or stop an alcoholic parent from drinking. It only gives the teen a whole new set of problems.

Many young people find it difficult to succeed on their own under the best of circumstances. Even college graduates may

The problems that runaway teens encounter—such as homelessness—may be more difficult than those they were trying to escape.

have a hard time finding a job that pays enough to support themselves. Imagine what it would be like to try to find work without a high school diploma or work experience. Within a few days of leaving home, most runaways are forced to turn to sex or drugs for survival.

"I ran out of money in about two weeks," said Gary, a runaway who has been on the streets for six months. "I had heard about this guy that wanted to look at young guys, and he'd give them money for posing for him. I thought it was gross, but after a week or so of eating out of restaurant dumpsters, I figured, how bad could it be? Besides, most of the kids I met were either selling drugs or their bodies."

Life on the run is dangerous and can be fatal. Runaways who have sex with strangers or who share drug needles are at especially high risk of catching hepatitis or AIDS. Even when they're not selling sex or drugs, runaways don't get adequate medical care. On the streets, what might otherwise be a routine medical problem can become life threatening. Like homeless adults, homeless teens are often victims of violent crime. Or they feel they have run out of options and take their own lives. Each year, about 5,000 runaways die from illness, assault, and suicide.

A Way Out

A number of national organizations operate toll-free hot lines that runaways can call for help. Staffed by trained volunteers, they offer several important services. These include:

■ Message relays

■ Referrals for shelter, transportation, and medical care

■ Support and referrals for teens at risk of running away

■ Crisis intervention for teens who are depressed, suicidal, and/or being abused

These hot lines operate 24 hours a day, 365 days a year. To reach these hot lines, call:

National Runaway Switchboard—1-800-621-4000; in Chicago, 1-800-621-3230; for hearing impaired, 1-800-621-0394.

Runaway Hot Line—1-800-231-6946; in Texas, 1-800-392-3352.

What happens when a teen calls a runaway hot line depends on what the teen wants. The hot-line volunteer's main concern is the teen's safety. The organizations maintain databases of thousands of resources around the country, including runaway shelters, medical facilities, social service agencies, and support groups. They use these to find help near the caller's location.

The volunteer will get some basic information from the teen, but it is all confidential. If a caller just wants to send a message home, the volunteer will get a parent or guardian's name and phone number and enough information to identify the runaway to the family. The teen can call back later to receive a message from home. His or her exact location isn't asked, and calls aren't traced. Many runaways have been reunited with their families through this neutral communication link. Sometimes hot lines can arrange conference calls to parents or to shelters and other agencies.

National organizations such as the National Runaway Switchboard and the Runaway Hot Line receive an average of 200 calls a day from troubled teens. The average age of callers is 15, although they receive calls from children as young as 9 years old.

"I was afraid to call home," said Lucas, a 16-year-old who ran away after his parents divorced. "I left after my mom and I had a really big fight. I figured that my dad would be so mad, he'd kill me.

"I was crashing in a park with three or four other kids who had left home," he recalled. "One morning I woke up to find my wallet was gone—not that there was that much in it. I realized I couldn't trust any of these people who called themselves my friends. I felt at the end of my rope, and I called a runaway hot line. I had seen the number on the bulletin board in the bus station. The volunteer told me about a shelter nearby."

Through the volunteer, Lucas let his mom know that he was safe in a runaway shelter and that he would like to come home. The next day he called the hot line, and a message was waiting for him. A ticket home was waiting at the bus station.

"My dad was mad at me for a long time," Lucas said. "I think it was his way of dealing with being so scared when I was gone. Mom cried a lot, like she couldn't believe I was really home. It was weird, because before I left, I didn't even think they'd miss me."

Facing Problems Head-On

Running away is a last resort. Teens aren't running *to* something, they are running from an intolerable situation. Organizations for runaways can help teens after they've left home, but they would rather save teens and their families from the pain of running away.

Runaway hot lines aren't just for runaways. They help any teen who needs someone to listen or who needs to find help for a problem. They can help put teens in touch with a wide range of local resources that can prevent a problem from turning into a crisis. Other school and community resources are available, too.

Broken families, sexual abuse, alcoholic parents, and emotional isolation all are serious and painful problems that some teens face. It's tempting to run away from them, but running doesn't solve anything, and it can put the teen in even greater physical and emotional danger. Sometimes a home environment is so bad that a change is the only solution, but the answer isn't on the streets. It may be with relatives or friends, a foster home, or a youth shelter. Teens need to locate and rely on the community resources available to help them resolve their family problems successfully.

Interview

Karyn was in nursing school when her brother committed suicide ten years ago. Although her family would not talk about it for many years, they are now active in a support group for survivors. In this interview, Karyn described how she came to terms with her brother's death.

My brother took his life when he was 17. I was 19 at the time. We were very close. We used to spend a lot of time out in the backyard on summer nights talking. We'd talk about our problems and about the future.

Our family had its problems. We weren't good at communicating with each other. My father worked a lot, so he wasn't around much. When he was, a lot of times he would judge us without hearing the other side of the story. Tim and I would protect each other. A lot of the time, my mom's ability to deal with family problems was not all that good.

I don't think we were that unusual. I saw the same things going on in a lot of my friends' families. I had only one friend who had a very open relationship with her family, and I envied that a lot.

Anyway, Tim and I stuck together. We were the middle two of four kids. When we were teens, we didn't know where to go or what to do. We could talk to friends, but that's just getting things off your chest. It's not getting answers.

Tim had started having some problems in sixth grade. When he was in eighth grade, my parents tried to get him help, but he resisted. They sent him to a private therapist, but he wouldn't talk. The therapist told my parents to stop wasting their money. They must have been pretty frustrated, and things didn't get any better.

Toward the end of his life, it seemed that Tim and my father were at odds all the time. I didn't really know how unhappy Tim was.

Things were so bad between Tim and my dad that the year before I went away to college Tim moved out of the house and went to live with some friends. I think physically removing himself was his way of letting go of the family. It made it hard for us to spend time together to talk. After he killed himself, I kept thinking, maybe if I had been around. . . .

The teenage years were just a horrible, awful time—for my family, anyway. I wrote to Tim when I went away to college. I told him that life isn't the same after high school—that things get better. He had gone to live with another family, with two boys he was friends with. They told me he would reread my letters over and over. They meant a lot to him.

Tim was an artist and perfectionist. If he didn't like what he was drawing, he would crumple it up. You'd always walk in and see all these balls of paper he had thrown away.

He closed up more and more toward the time he died.

He distanced himself. He didn't write or call. I was so busy with school, I didn't notice it, but I think he knew what he was going to do.

It's strange, because we had the same background and the same problems. But I have a very persevering personality. He'd never give himself a break, and if something went wrong for him, it was the end of the world. I don't think he ever realized that you could get through, and things could get better.

My brother killed himself with someone else. They made a tape together, talking about everything that was wrong with their lives and why they were so unhappy, but I never heard it. My parents arranged for the police to impound it so no one would hear it. At first I was angry about that. I used to dream about hearing the tape, but now I don't think I want to hear it.

When it happened, I was visiting my grandparents. My grandmother answered the phone when it rang, then got this look on her face and motioned for me to come over. She gave the phone to me, and my mother said, "Tim's dead." I called her a liar, and I screamed and screamed. I flipped out.

I was in nursing school at the time. I took a leave of absence for a week. When I came back, I was crying all through classes. One of my instructors said, "What are you crying about? You should be over that by now." She said if I couldn't handle stress, I probably shouldn't be a nurse. That did zero for my self-esteem.

I didn't have a support system. Mom and Dad didn't cope with Tim's death very well. They couldn't handle my being emotional. I was very alone. I think in many families where teens commit suicide there wasn't a lot of support to begin with.

When a kid commits suicide, most of the attention is on the parents. A lot of times the kids get left out. I felt very left out. My friends tried to help for a while. But unless you've had someone in your family kill themselves, it's very difficult to understand. My friends couldn't begin to understand where I was coming from.

When Tim committed suicide, he took away all the things I dreamed of—sharing the important occasions of our lives. I was very angry at him for leaving me, and for leaving me without the support I had from him.

I was angry at the school, too—at the art teacher who belittled him for what he drew. He drew morbid things. If anybody had bothered to really look into it, they would have seen the pain he was in. Instead, the art teacher criticized him and said he was wasting his talent.

I blamed myself and I blamed him. I mostly blamed my parents for a long time. When you're a kid, you think everything hangs on them. Now that I have kids of my own, I understand that when you're a parent, you just do the best you can.

The pain of suicide is so great that for some people it's easier not to remember. For a while, we didn't talk about Tim at family gatherings. It was like he never existed. It's amazing how much my family has changed since then, but it's taken us ten years.

It's so hard. You have to stop feeling responsible when you're not. And for a teen survivor, it's easy to lose your sense of reality. I just can't tell you what suicide does to brothers and sisters. I don't think you can ever find a normal life after that. It stunted me for a few years. I felt I wasn't good, because I wasn't good enough to stop him. It's affected my whole life. I always want to be in control. I never want to be out of control like that again.

It forces you to see that life can end. I had nightmares for a while. I was afraid to get in cars, because I thought I would have an accident and die. For a while, I thought I would never have a normal life.

I really wanted Tim to be at my wedding; I really wanted him to be an uncle. I wish my kids could meet him. I think how much they are missing by not having him in their lives. That's what you can never get back. It ended life for me for a while to lose him.

I wondered why him and not me? Every one of us feels awkward and inadequate in some ways. I always looked at him and his talent and envied him. He always had more friends than I did. People loved him. He had a lot more going for him than I did. It still mystifies me. He obviously didn't feel there was anything positive about his life. It was such a waste of a wonderful, vibrant, talented person. If he had just been able to see he had so much to offer. That's what really hurts, the waste of a life.

Sometimes people don't think of what they leave behind. As a nurse, I see a lot of young people brought back from suicide attempts. The families come in, and you see their faces, and you just know how hurt and angry they are. A lot of young people just don't see a future. The only thing I can say is talk, talk, talk. Teens should find an adult they trust. There's one there somewhere. Like Tim's friend's mother, where he lived that last year. He opened up to her, but I think by then it was too late. If he had found her sooner, maybe things would have turned around for him.

A lot of depressed teens don't talk—they withdraw. Even if they seem to have a lot of friends, they don't open up that much. Sometimes teens in trouble aren't that obvious—like the kid with my brother. He always made really sarcastic remarks, but if you weren't in tune, you'd miss it. It was a subtle nastiness. You just knew he was unhappy and wanted everybody else to be. But he knew how to play it. He did well in school. His parents were blind . . . they just didn't see behind the sarcasm.

It took my parents a couple of years to catch on that something wasn't right with Tim. It was easier for me to see that something wasn't right than it was for my parents. You keep secrets from your parents.

I get so angry when kids say that life isn't worth living. There is no teenager who has done enough living to know that. These kids don't know what life is.

CHAPTER 7

The Pain of Suicide

Q A kid in my English class shot and killed himself the other day. I still can't believe it. He was kind of quiet, but nobody thought anything was wrong. How were we supposed to know? I can't get it out of my mind.

A Few events have as much of an emotional impact on teens as the suicide of a classmate, friend, brother, or sister. In fact, sometimes one teen's suicide will lead to others in the same community. It's hard to sort out your feelings after a tragedy like this. You feel shocked and shaken and upset by the loss. At the same time, you might feel guilty that you weren't able to prevent the suicide or fearful for your own state of mind. Don't be surprised if you get angry at the boy who killed himself. It's a natural reaction to this kind of loss. It helps to acknowledge all your feelings and to talk about them with your friends, your parents, or a teacher you trust. Often, after a teen suicide, the school makes counseling available for students who feel they need help understanding their emotions.

It's important to realize that you were not responsible for the suicide in any way. Your classmate made the decision to pull the trigger; he took his own life. At that point, you couldn't have stopped him, even if you did know what he was planning. Although some suicide victims plainly signal their intentions, many others hide their plans. Those who don't talk about their plans are usually more intent on dying.

Suicide is one of the leading causes of death among young people in the United States. Only accidents and homicides claim more young lives. No one type of person commits suicide more than another. It touches girls as well as boys, good students and bad, rich and poor. It doesn't have anything to do with how popular a person is or how much the teen seems to have going for him or her.

The one thing all teens who commit suicide have in common is that they are in tremendous emotional pain. Some choose suicide because they see it as the only way to end that pain. Others may see suicide as a way of getting revenge on the person whom they blame for their pain. For many others, a suicide attempt is a cry for help, a way of letting the world know that they are in pain. Unfortunately, if the suicide is accomplished, no one can help.

Teens need to learn other ways to cope with painful feelings of sadness, loss, anger, guilt, or unworthiness. These are powerful, sometimes overwhelming, emotions. With support, however, teens can learn to bring them under control and lessen the pain.

Danger Signs of Suicide

When a teen commits suicide, the first reaction among friends and family is usually shock. Most people—teens and adults—feel pain at different points throughout their lifetime, but they don't commit suicide. It is often very difficult for them to imagine anyone being in enough pain to want to die. But when the survivors take time to look back at the suicide victim's life, sometimes they can remember signs that the person was very unhappy. In some cases, the suicide victim even lets his or her intentions be known ahead of time.

We've already talked about some of the signs of depression.

Suicide is the third leading cause of death among young people in the United States. Many of these tragic deaths are more a plea for help than a wish to die.

These include moodiness, pessimism, withdrawal, changes in eating or sleeping habits, or loss of interest in friends or hobbies. Depressed people are likely to have thoughts of suicide, although most do not act on them. Still, it's important for depressed people to get help.

When a person becomes suicidal, it's critical to get help as soon as possible. How can you know if someone is suicidal? Someone is probably thinking seriously of suicide if he or she:

Is preoccupied with death;

Talks about hurting him- or herself or has already done so;

Says he or she would be better off dead;

Has a weapon, pills, or other means of committing suicide;

Suddenly seems happy or relieved after a long depression;

Makes a will or gives away possessions.

About 80 percent of people who commit suicide tell someone about their plans to hurt themselves before they do it. If you think someone you know is suicidal, try to get him or her to talk about it. Find out what is troubling that person. Try to get help as well. A suicide prevention hot line is a good resource. Hot-line volunteers are trained to listen and to talk the person through the crisis. They then can provide referrals for further counseling.

"When Bennie broke up with me last year, I wanted to die," said Rosemarie, 17. "People kept telling me that things would get better and that I'd have lots of other boyfriends. It didn't matter. I kept feeling worse and worse. I thought if I killed myself, at least he'd see how much I really loved him and how much he hurt me."

Rosemarie planned to cut her wrists one evening when her parents would be out to dinner. That day at lunch, she gave her favorite bracelet to her best friend. "Tina knew right away that something was up," Rosemarie said. "She talked about how important our friendship was to her and how awful it would be if I weren't around. Then she got me to call a teen hot line, and they helped me find a therapist."

If you yourself are beginning to think of suicide, talk to someone. Seek out a friend or call a suicide prevention hot line and talk to someone until you can get your feelings back under control. Do it right away, and don't worry about what time it is. Although you may feel as though you want to be alone, being alone can be dangerous when you're in this state of mind. Also be aware that serious thoughts of suicide are a pretty sure sign of deep depression, for which you will need to seek professional help.

If you actually see someone who is in the process of hurting him- or herself, or is incoherent or unconscious, get immediate help. Call an adult you trust, the police, an ambulance, or the nearest hospital emergency room. Stay with the person until help arrives.

Recovery

Many more teens attempt suicide than accomplish it. Generally, more boys tend to succeed on the first attempt than do girls. That may be because boys most often use more effective means of killing themselves, such as guns.

Some people who attempt suicide don't really want to die, but they do want help. Others believe that they want to die, but don't know how to kill themselves. Regardless of why, some people who attempt suicide get another chance at life. A few will attempt suicide again and again until they eventually do take their lives. The rest begin to walk the long road back from darkness.

Many people who are discovered in the process of, or soon after, attempting suicide are first taken to the hospital emergency room. There, medical professionals can take the necessary steps to save the person's life. The person will stay in the hospital until his or her medical condition is stabilized.

Most states require that any person who attempts suicide undergo psychiatric evaluation and treatment. This is to ensure that the person is unlikely to try suicide again. Initial treatment can last from a few weeks to a few months, depending on the person's condition. This treatment may take place in the psychiatric ward of a general hospital or at a private psychiatric hospital. Some private hospitals have special units for treating emotionally disturbed teens.

The person may be put on medication, usually for six months or longer. He or she will be interviewed and evaluated by one or more mental health professionals, who will then develop an appropriate treatment program. This program may involve individual counseling and group sessions with other patients. Very often family counseling is involved.

"The last people I wanted to talk to were my mom and dad. I mean, they didn't even talk to each other half the time. But my doctor said it was important, so I went along with it," said

Hector, who had been hospitalized after a suicide attempt during his freshman year in high school. "It was hard for me, but I think it was even harder for them."

With the help of a counselor, Hector and his parents were able to express a lot of feelings that they had tried to ignore. Hector's father, who had grown up in a poor neighborhood of Los Angeles, realized how much pressure he had been putting on his son to succeed in school sports. And Hector came to understand that the problems in his parents' marriage were not his fault.

"They got divorced about three years later. That was a hard time for me, too, but I knew I'd survive with counseling," said Hector. "At the time of the divorce, I knew enough to go for help."

After hospitalization, follow-up care and counseling may last for a year or more until the patient readjusts to the pressures of life outside the hospital. He or she may continue to take medication for depression. Talk therapy usually continues. At first, sessions may take place several times a week. They usually become less frequent as the person regains emotional strength. At any time the person feels bad, he or she may decide to make more frequent visits to a counselor. In times of crisis—such as when Hector's parents divorced—many people find it helpful to go back to counseling for support, even if they no longer go for therapy regularly.

Adjustments

The hospital environment is structured to help the recovering patient gain coping skills through individual therapy and group interactions. The patient is surrounded by people who want to help him or her get well and who are trained to do so. This isn't necessarily true in the world outside the hospital. The person's problems don't go away while he or she is in the hospital—he or she just gets new tools to deal with them. And the teen who is returning to school after attempting suicide may face new obstacles as well.

Depression and suicide are still very misunderstood. Some people feel uncomfortable with someone who has attempted suicide. Others may be very curious and want to know more details than the person wants to share.

"I found out who my friends were," said Carmen, who attempted suicide at 17. "My best friend stuck by me and came to see me in the hospital and everything. So did this other girl, Sandy, who I was friends with before, but I never thought we were that close. When I got back to school, they both really helped me get back into things.

"I also stayed in touch with a boy I met at the hospital. He was the only one who really understood what I was going through. A lot of other people I thought I was tight with avoided me. I wasn't mad, because I know they didn't know what to say and they felt awkward. I saw the same thing happen to a

Coping with emotional pain is easier when you can share your feelings with someone who cares.

guy in my class who had been diagnosed as having cancer," Carmen continued.

Carmen says she is glad to talk about her experience with anyone who asks. "At first I didn't, because it was too painful. But when I did say something, I found out that a lot of kids I talked to had felt the same way I had at one time or another. I figured that if I could save them and their families some of the pain I went through, it would be worth it."

Carmen was lucky. She got a chance to learn from her experience. Thousands of teens each year don't get a second chance. They may put an end to their own pain, but they cause tremendous suffering among surviving family and friends.

It sounds easy to say that nothing is so bad that it's worth dying for, and that everything gets better over time, but it's only partially true. Many situations improve over time; and, with experience, most people become better able to deal with the problems in their lives. Although talking to others about your feelings won't always take away the pain, it makes it easier to handle when you share the burden with someone who cares about you.

Many resources are available to help teens cope with depression and other emotional problems. Some of them are discussed in detail in Chapter 1, "Communicating" and Chapter 4, "Reaching Out." Teens can turn to friends, family, people at school, community hospitals, mental health clinics, and many other sources of help.

Local phone books have listings of state, county, and other agencies that can help teens. Some phone books group such agencies under the label "Human Services" in a special section. You can also look under such headings as "Alcohol and Drug Abuse," "Children and Youth" or "Family Services," "Mental Health," "Self-Help Support Groups," and "Suicide."

The Yellow Pages list private hospitals and organizations under similar headings. Psychologists and psychiatrists are listed in the Yellow Pages as well. In addition, community hospitals can also provide names of mental health care specialists.

Local newspapers often carry listings of self-help groups for depression, suicide, substance abuse, eating disorders, family problems, and many other issues that affect teens. These groups include Alateen, for teens with an alcoholic parent, and Survivors of Suicide.

Other agencies that can provide information are listed below.

National Organizations

National Institute of Mental
  Health (NIMH)
Public Inquiries
Room 15C-05
5600 Fishers Lane
Rockville, MD 20857
(800) 421-4211 (301) 443-4513
  NIMH sponsors the
  Depression Awareness,
  Recognition and Treatment
  (D/ART) program based on
  more than 40 years of
  research on the diagnosis
  and treatment of depression.
  They also publish a variety of
materials on depression and
other mental health problems. A few of special
interest to teens are the
following:
- What to Do When a Friend Is
  Depressed: A Guide for
  Students
- Plain Talk About Depression
- Let's Talk About Depression
- D/ART Fact Sheet

National Mental Health
  Association
1021 Prince St.
Alexandria, VA 22314
(703) 684-7222

Suicide Information and
    Education Centre (Canada)
1615 Tenth Avenue, SW
Calgary, AB T3C 0J7
(403) 245-3900

Hot Lines

Adolescent Suicide Hot
    Line/National Runaway
    Switchboard
(800) 621-4000
24 hours, every day

Alcohol and Drug and
    Treatment Information
    Services (Canada)
(800) 821-4357

Canadian Mental Health
    Association
(613) 737-7791

Cocaine Hot Line
(800) COCAINE
(800) 262-2463

National Runaway Hot Line
(800) 231-6946
in Texas (800) 392-3352
24 hours, every day

For More Information

An asterisk (*) indicates a young adult book.

Nonfiction
*Anonymous. *Go Ask Alice*. Prentice-Hall, 1971.
*Coombs, Samm H. *Teenage Survival Manual: How to Reach 20 in One Piece*. Monroe Press, 1989.
Elchoness, Monte. *Why Can't Anyone Hear Me?* Discovery Books, 1989.
*Frank, Anne. *The Diary of a Young Girl*. Doubleday, 1967.
*Gardner, G. *Teenage Suicide*. Simon & Schuster, 1990.
Giovaedini, P. L. *The Urge to Die: Why Young People Commit Suicide*. Macmillan, 1981.
Spungen, Deborah. *And I Don't Want to Live This Life*. Ballantine Books, 1983.
Styron, William. *Darkness Visible*. Random House, 1990.

Fiction
Green, Hannah. *I Never Promised You a Rose Garden*. Signet, 1964.
Guest, Judith. *Ordinary People*. Ballantine Books, 1976.
*Hinton, S. E. *The Outsiders*. Viking Press, 1967.
Miller, Sue. *Family Pictures*. Harper & Row, 1990.
Plath, Sylvia. *The Bell Jar*. Bantam Books, 1972.
*Salinger, J. D. *The Catcher in the Rye*. Bantam Books, 1964.
*Voigt, Cynthia. *A Solitary Blue*. Scholastic, 1983.

Movies
The following movies are available on VHS format.
The Breakfast Club, 1984.
Dead Poets Society, 1990.
Lost Angels, 1989.
Ordinary People, 1980.
The Outsiders, 1983.
St. Elmo's Fire, 1985.
Tough Love, 1985. [Aimed at parents]
Where the Day Takes You, 1992.

INDEX

Addictive substances, 48, 50. *See also* Substance abuse
Adolescence
  changes during, 22-23, 28
  conflicts during, 24-26
  health needs during, 28-29
  pressures during, 26-27
  relationships with friends during, 23-24
Alateen, 41
Alcohol use, 48, 50-51. *See also* Substance abuse
Alcoholics Anonymous, 48
Anger
  understanding your, 17
  ways to express, 15, 26, 27
Anorexia, 52-53
Antidepressants, 43-44
Athletics, 28-29

Biochemistry, 6, 34-35
Bulimia, 53-54

Caffeine, 48
Cigarette smoking, 48
Communicating
  confronting problems through, 20-21, 27, 73-74, 76
  with parents, 22, 35
  your feelings, 14, 15, 19
Community service, 29
Counselors. *See also* Guidance counselors
  benefits of talking with, 37, 54
  at runaway hot lines, 55-56

Death. *See also* Suicide
  depression resulting from friend or family member's, 35
  talk about, 33-34
Depression
  causes of, 34-36
  facts about, 13, 30-31
  as illness, 38
  interview discussing, 6-11
  signs of, 31-34, 37, 69-70
  substance abuse and, 47-48
  treatment of, 42-45
  types of, 6, 32
Diaries, 18
Diet, 28

Eating disorders, 51-54
Emotions. *See* Feelings
Endorphins, 28
Environment, 35
Exercise, 28

Families. *See also* Parents
  abusive situations in, 56-57
  as support network, 19, 27, 39-40
Feelings
  sorting out your, 14-19, 21
  talking to someone you trust about your, 19, 21, 26, 29, 74-75
  ways to express, 14-16, 54
Frank, Anne, 18
Friends
  during adolescence, 23-24
  as support network, 19, 27, 39-40, 74

Grades, 26-27
Guidance counselors, 19, 41-42. See also Counselors

Homelessness, 59. *See also* Runaways
Hot lines
  for help with problems, 46
  listing of, 77
  runaway, 55, 56, 60, 61

Jobs, and runaways, 58-59

Letter writing, to express feelings, 18
Listening, 21

Major depression, 32. *See also* Depression

Manic-depressive illness, 6, 32. *See also* Depression

Medications, 43-44

Mental health professionals
benefits of seeing, 38-39
types of, 42-45

Minor depression, 32. *See also* Depression

Mood swings, 30-31

Narcotics Anonymous, 48

National organizations
to help runaways, 59-60
listing of, 76-77

National Runaway Switchboard, 60

Nicotine, 48

Overeating, 51-52

Parents. *See also* Families
communicating with, 22, 27, 35, 57
conflict with, 25-26, 56-57, 61
running away from, 55-56
as support network, 27, 39-40

Personality, 35-36

Problems
communicating about your, 14-16
confronting your, 20-21, 51, 61
sorting out your feelings about, 16-19
talking to someone your trust about your, 19, 57

Psychiatric hospitals, 8-9, 72, 73

Psychiatrists
description of, 42-44
working with people who attempted suicide, 72

Psychologists
description of, 44-45
talking about your feelings to, 17

Psychotherapy, 43

Relationships
conflict in, 24-26

with friends, 23-24, 39-40
with opposite sex, 24
with parents, 22-23, 25-26, 35, 36, 39-40, 55-57, 66, 72-73. *See also* Parents

Relaxation techniques, 45

Runaway Hot Line, 60

Runaways
family situations of, 56-57
options for, 55-56, 59-61
problems facing, 57, 59

School
pressure over performance in, 26-27, 35, 36
resources at, 40-42

Self-esteem
from being loved, 39
benefits of good, 27
role of, 36-37
unhappiness resulting from low, 54

Sleep, 28

Smoking, 48

Snacks, 28

Social workers, 45

Sports, 28-29

Stress, 44

Substance abuse
depression and, 47-48
effects of, 48, 50
recovery from, 54

Suicide
danger signs of, 33-34, 69-70
facts about, 12, 13, 69-71
interview about, 62-67
recovery from attempted, 72-73
substance abuse and thoughts of, 50

Support groups, 46

Teachers
blaming problems on, 36
talking about problems with, 19, 27, 40-41

Tutoring, 27

Volunteering, 29